It's Time for School, Charlie Brown

LITTLE SIMON
An imprint of Simon & Schuster Children's Publishing Division
1230 Avenue of the Americas, New York, New York 10020
Copyright © 2002 United Feature Syndicate, Inc. All rights reserved. PEANUTS is a registered trademark of
United Feature Syndicate, Inc.
All rights reserved, including the right of reproduction in whole or in part in any form.
READY-TO-READ, LITTLE SIMON, and colophon are registered trademarks of Simon & Schuster.
Printed in Mexico
First Edition
2 4 6 8 10 9 7 5 3 1

The library edition of this book has been cataloged by the Library of Congress.
ISBN 0-689-85147-2 (Lib. ed.)
ISBN 0-689-85146-4 (Pbk.)

It's Time for School, Charlie Brown

Based on the comic strips
by Charles M. Schulz
Adapted by Judy Katschke
Art adapted by Peter and Nick LoBianco

Ready-to-Read

Little Simon

New York   London   Toronto   Sydney   Singapore

Poor Charlie Brown!
He couldn't kick a football.
Or pitch a decent baseball.
Or even fly a kite.
But when it came to worrying about
school—he was the world champ!

"Vacation is almost over!" Charlie
 Brown's little sister, Sally, said.
"Schooltime will soon be rolling around!"
 Charlie Brown sighed.
"Schooltime doesn't roll around,"
 he said. "It leaps right out at you!"

7

"You look kind of down, Charlie Brown,"
   Linus said.
"I worry about school a lot,"
   Charlie Brown said.
"And I worry about my worrying so
   much about school!"

Charlie Brown decided to get help—
from Lucy!
"Okay, what's your problem?"
Lucy asked.
"*Tomorrow!*" Charlie Brown said.
"I am worrying about tomorrow. Then
when tomorrow becomes today, I start
worrying about tomorrow again!"

"I think I can help you, Charlie Brown,"
Lucy said. "Now, the first thing you
have to do is turn around!"
Charlie Brown turned around.

"Throw out your chest and face the future!"
Lucy shouted.
"Now raise your arm and clench your fist!"
Charlie Brown did what Lucy told him to do.

Suddenly Charlie Brown wasn't
worried about school anymore!
He might ace every pop quiz! He might
become hall monitor! He might even
talk to the Little Red-Haired Girl! Or—
"You look ridiculous!" Lucy said.
—he might not!

Soon after school started, a spelling
contest was announced.
"They're going to have a spelling bee?"
Charlie Brown asked.

I should enter it, Charlie Brown thought.
That's the sort of thing I need to give me
confidence and self-esteem!

I think I'll raise my hand and
volunteer, Charlie Brown decided.
It will be good for me!
He tried to raise his hand.

But . . .
"My hand won't go up," Charlie Brown
groaned to himself. "It's smarter than I am!"

Charlie Brown *did* enter the spelling bee.
But when his friends found out,
they did not exactly cheer him on.
"You're crazy!" Lucy whispered.
"Don't do it. You'll just make a fool
of yourself!"

"*You?!*" Lucy cried. "You're going to enter
   the citywide spelling bee? You??"
   Charlie Brown threw his hands up in the air.
"I can *try*, can't I?" Charlie Brown
   asked. "What's the good of living if you
   don't try a few things?"

Lucy leaned over to Charlie Brown.
"Spell 'Acetylcholinesterase'!"
"Maybe I shouldn't enter," Charlie Brown
gulped.

But as the spelling bee got nearer
and nearer, Charlie Brown got braver.
"Nobody thinks I can win the citywide
spelling bee, Snoopy,"
Charlie Brown told his dog.
"But I'm going to show them!"

"I have trouble remembering:
  I before *B* except after *T*?"
  Charlie Brown said,
"Or is it *V* before *Z* except after *E*?"
  Good grief, thought Snoopy!

I guess I really don't have to worry,
Charlie Brown thought. All the words
in the first round are easy.
The kid before me got an easy one.
I feel strangely calm. Charlie Brown
waited for his turn.

"Maze?" Charlie Brown repeated.
"Yes, ma'am. That's an easy one."
Charlie Brown wasn't worried.
He smiled. He took a deep breath.
And he began to spell . . . "M-A-Y-S!"

Charlie Brown blew it!
Soon he was back at his desk.
Worrying!
What would his friends say?
What would Snoopy do?

"Yes, ma'am?" Charlie Brown answered
his teacher when she called his name.
"Why did I have my head on my desk?
You don't know? You're asking me
why I had my head on my desk?"

"Because I blew the spelling bee!!!"
Charlie Brown yelled at the top
of his lungs. "That's why!"

"Oh, good grief!" Charlie Brown gasped.
"Now I've done it!"
It was the worst day of
Charlie Brown's life.
He woke up looking forward
to the spelling bee.

And he ended up in the principal's office!
"On a day like this," Charlie Brown sighed,
"a person really needs his faithful dog
to come running out to greet him!"

But Snoopy was busy.

Poor Charlie Brown!
He couldn't kick a football.
Or pitch a decent baseball.
Or even fly a kite.
And now he couldn't even spell!

GOOD GRIEF!!